It's Not As Bad As You *Think*

It's Not As Bad As You *Think*

(Coping With Upset Feelings)

by A. Jack Hafner, Ph.D.

First published, January 1981

Copyright© 1981 by Hazelden Foundation. All rights reserved. No part of this book may be reproduced without the written permission of the publisher.

ISBN: 0-89486-116-6

Printed in the United States of America.

Editor's Note:
Hazelden Educational Materials offers a variety of information on chemical dependency and related areas. Our publications do not necessarily represent Hazelden or its programs, nor do they officially speak for any Twelve Step organization.

Introduction

What causes people to become upset? What we tell ourselves! Our *thinking* about something, not the something itself, upsets us. *No situation or person can upset us or make us feel bad.* We are responsible for causing our feelings. Thus, when we judge or evaluate something in a negative way, we will usually be upset. In contrast, when we judge or evaluate something in a positive way, we will usually feel good. Our first basic point is: *people are not upset by things but by their thinking about those things.*

To illustrate this very important point, let's look at the following examples. Bill and Bob are standing in their apartments looking out the window at an approaching thunderstorm. Bob becomes very anxious, closes the drapes and turns up the radio as loud as possible to drown out the sights and sounds which frighten him. Bill, however, excitedly takes his camera from the closet, sets it up on a tripod and takes pictures of the unusually brilliant flashes of lightning. He has wanted to get pictures of a thunderstorm like this for some time. The feelings of neither man were brought about by the thunderstorm itself, but by the way he judged the situation.

*The approach used in this pamphlet is based on the work of Albert Ellis and his Rational Emotive Therapy.

To further illustrate this point, let's look at another situation. Jean and Jim are sitting in their office and the boss walks by without saying "Hello." Jim looks up and says to himself, "I wonder what I did wrong today?" He feels upset for the rest of the day worrying about what he might have done wrong. Jean, on the other hand, looks up at the boss walking by in silence and says "I wonder what's wrong with the boss today?" She goes on with her work, no longer thinking about the situation. This situation, common to two individuals, resulted in different reactions based upon how each evaluated the situation. In other words, *we feel the way we think*. The more upset we are, the more upsetting or negative our thinking is likely to be.

What happens as a result of our feelings? Actions. What we do generally depends on how we feel about a particular situation. When we get angry, we might yell at someone. When we get depressed, we might withdraw. An upset person often acts in self-defeating ways. For instance, many people use alcohol or other drugs to change their angry or depressed feelings. With enough experience using mood-altering substances to change feelings, an individual may begin to believe "I need a drink to feel better."

Let's look again at the previous examples to see how Bob and Jim might have responded to their situations. Bob might have taken a drink or drugs to calm his nerves and reduce his anxiety. Because his boss ignored him, Jim might have brooded the rest of the day and then stopped off at a bar on his way home for a drink to lift his spirits. Using alcohol or drugs can become a way of dealing with upset feelings thus fostering a dependency on mood-altering substances.

What has been emphasized up to this point is that *we feel the way we think* and we act accordingly. Generally, people with alcohol or other drug problems have learned to use alcohol or other drugs as a way of trying to deal with their upsetting feelings. However, there are other ways to change upset feelings. The ABC format is one method.

The ABC format helps us understand how our beliefs or thinking about a situation causes our feelings and what we can do about those feelings. It is a procedure that can be used to take a personal inventory. The format will clarify our problems in regard to upset feelings.

In the ABC format, "A" stands for the activating event or the situation about which a person has emotional feelings. The "B" stands for the belief system or thoughts that an individual has about the situation. Put another way, "B" is what you tell yourself in regard to the situation. "C" stands for the emotional consequences or feelings that you're having in regard to the situation (A). As stated previously, when you judge or evaluate a situation negatively, then you will usually feel upset, maybe depressed, anxious or angry.

The next part of the ABC format is "C_b," which stands for consequential behavior, the way you act or behave as a result of your emotional feelings. Strong upset feelings often result in overreaction, which is a negative consequence. Our overreaction will probably be self-defeating or destructive behavior.

Since the ABC format can help us understand what happens in problem situations, let's look at an example: Your spouse criticizes you (A). You think (B) "He or she *should not* have criticized me, I *must* be right." Your feeling (C) is strong anger. The consequential behavior (C_b) is yelling at your spouse and then getting high on alcohol or other drugs. Thus the format, used in this way, is helpful for understanding a problem situation and your thoughts, feelings, and reactions to it.

Common Upsetting Thinking

Examination of the thinking (B) that makes you feel upset (C) generally reveals that certain ideas tend to be particularly upsetting. Most upsetting thinking reflects the attitudes underlying "awful," "I can't," and "should."

The attitude behind the word "awful" is almost always an unrealistic exaggeration. When we "awfulize," we tend to change disappointments or difficulties into disasters. "Wouldn't it be *awful* if I didn't get promoted?" Such thinking usually makes an unfortunate or difficult situation worse. The more upset we find ourselves, the more we are likely to be exaggerating the unfortunate aspect of a situation.

Related to "awfulizing" is the attitude expressed in the words, "I can't." When we say to ourselves, "I can't," we tend to change something that is difficult into something impossible! There are two categories of "I can't." One is the "I can't stand it" category. You think you can't bear, stand, or tolerate something. For example, "I can't stand people being late" or "I can't stand my kids talking back to me." The other category is "I can't do it," such as "I can't do any better," "I can't do anything right," "I can't change."

Next, let's look at the troublesome "shoulds" which are almost always unrealistic, absolute demands. When we tell ourselves we "should" do something, we change desires into demands. "Should" means I absolutely must have things my way. We demand that we do well and receive others' approval. We demand that other people treat us fairly.

"Should" may also imply an undoing, that is, we demand that things be different than they are. For example, "It shouldn't be raining," or "You shouldn't have criticized me." These are unrealistic demands or expectations that feed our resentments. We are *demanding* what we want, that the past be changed!

It has been said that this attempt to control may be the basis of much, if not most, of our emotional upset. When we demand, insist, or command that things *should* happen our way, but they don't, it is *awful*.

Evaluating our personal worth or the worth of others can also be upsetting. Downing, damning or blaming oneself or others is usually overgeneralizing. For instance, saying, "I am a bad person because of what I did" or "I am a loser" or "that person is no damn good," is upsetting thinking and certainly jumping to conclusions about a person's total worth. We disregard the fact that every one of us acts in both positive and negative ways. We disregard the fact that mistake-making is part of the human condition. It is inappropriate to conclude a person is "no damn good," if he/she makes a mistake or does something bad, but this is what we do with this kind of upsetting thinking.

Upset Feelings Mean Upsetting Thoughts

Because we feel the way we think, *upset feelings mean upsetting thoughts*. The degree of our emotional upset is a measure of how upsetting or negative our thinking is. Most people mistakenly believe emotional upset is caused by external pressures. People commonly believe that they have little ability to change their upset feelings until the external pressures or other people that "cause" the upset change. Some people also believe the way to temporarily change their upset feelings is through the use of mood-altering substances.

To blame other people or situations for our upset feelings gives a person an excuse to use alcohol or other drugs. In many situations the upset feelings are understandable. However, when we justify our upsets, then we do not look at the underlying distressing beliefs that are really causing the upset feelings. Our upsetting thinking is something over which we *do have control* in contrast to other people's behavior or problem situations. We are responsible for how we feel in regard to a situation primarily on the basis of what we think about that situation. Rather than trying to justify or blame the upset, the important question to ask is "What is the result of my getting upset?" If our emotional upset results in self-defeating or destructive behavior, then it would be better to do something constructive about our upset feelings. That's what the ABC format allows us to do. The ABCs are a form of personal inventory that helps people understand their problem situation (A); understand their negative thinking (B) about the situation; the emotional consequences (C) of this thinking, and their behavior (C_b).

Step 1 of AA and the ABCs

The ABC format may be related directly to the "powerlessness" and "unmanageability" of Step 1 of Alcoholics Anonymous. The alcohol or drug dependent person's non-acceptance of Step 1 relects the unrealistic and upsetting thinking (B) which is called denial. The denial of "powerlessness" reflects the upsetting belief of the *demand to control:* "I *should* be able to control my use of alcohol or other drugs." The consequences of such thinking are the upset feelings (C) of anger, guilt, anxiety, and depression when the demand to control is not being realized. The more we demand to control, the more emotionally upset we become. The behavioral consequences (C_b) of this emotional upset are likely to be self-defeating, destructive actions including getting drunk or high. The result of this unrealistic demand to control, or the denial of "powerlessness," makes our lives "unmanageable." The ABC format can help us regain self-respect and develop insight into our "powerlessness" and "unmanageability."

Bringing About Change in Feelings

Since our negative thinking causes our upset, we can modify our negative thinking to change our upset feelings. We bring about change by adding (D) to the ABCs.

"D" stands for disputing or questioning the thoughts (B) that are causing our upset feelings (C). It is the point where we talk ourselves out of being so upset. How do we talk ourselves out of being so upset? By asking the questions, "Why?" or "Who said so?" or "Where is my evidence?", and then answering the questions.

You question the reality of your "awfuls" and "I can'ts" by asking yourself "Who says it is awful?", "Why can't I?", or "Where is my evidence?" We might find that a situation is difficult, unfortunate or even very unpleasant, but it is unlikely that many things are truly *awful, impossible,* or *terrible.*

How do we question our demands or "shoulds"? By asking, "Why should it be?", "Who said so?", "Where is my evidence?" While it might be nicer if things did go our way, it is not *absolutely* necessary.

How do we put an end to our distressful self-downing or blaming? We do this by reminding ourselves that *everyone* makes mistakes.

One of the results of using the ABC process is self-acceptance. We learn not to rate ourselves or others as worthy or unworthy, but to accept the fact that we all behave in positive and negative ways. We learn to evaluate our *behavior* and not *ourselves*.

Step 2 of AA and the ABCs

As a way of learning to identify upsetting thinking (B) and then questioning (D) the negative thinking, it is very helpful to share worries and concerns with others. We are often so used to thinking in upsetting ways that it may be difficult at first to objectively view our thinking unless we ask for the assistance of another person. The sharing of thoughts with one's peers is also a way of putting into practice Step 2 of AA. Through the process of sharing with peers and modifying our thinking, we develop hope and realize the ability to change.

The Goal of ABCD

Up to this point, we have seen that our thinking (B) about situations (A) causes our feelings (C). When our thinking is upsetting, then our feelings are likely to be distressful, and when we are *very* upset, we often behave in ways that are self-defeating or harmful to others (C_b). Since our troubled thinking is the basis of our upset feeling, we need to modify this thinking by identifying and questioning (D) the rationale for our disturbing thoughts. Once we are able to modify our thinking, we will notice a decrease in the degree of our emotional upset. It is important to realize, however, that while the ABC process helps us reduce the intensity of our upset, it does not eliminate our emotional upset altogether. The goal of ABCD is not to do away with upset, but to *modify* the *amount* of distress a person experiences so that the individual is less likely to do destructive things or resort to alcohol or other drugs as a way of trying to change a mood or a feeling.

An Example of the ABCD Process

Applying the ABC format up to this point is as follows:
1) The situation (A): I'm going to a dinner party; my spouse is slow getting ready, and now we may be late for the party.
2) I'm feeling very angry (C).
3) I want to yell at her (C_b).
4) Here I take a personal inventory. I recognize and admit my anger and its consequences. What am I telling myself (B)? "My spouse *shouldn't* make me late." "I *must* have my way" (the need to control or self-centeredness).
5) Next, I start questioning (D) my upsetting thinking, my demandingness (B); "Who said my spouse should be on time?" "I said so." "Why should my spouse meet my expectations?" "Why must I have my way?" "Stop being so self-centered; stop trying to control!" Thus, I modify my upsetting thinking and as a result start to feel less upset.

The ABCs are a form of personal inventory. They help us understand that we feel the way we think and that if we want to change the way we feel, we must modify the way we think. We do not need to depend on alcohol or other drugs to change the way we feel.

The goal of A-D is to reduce our strong troubled feelings

so that they don't get in the way. We do not want to eliminate upset feelings altogether because emotional feelings, both negative and positive, are part of the human condition. However, the more negative our thinking gets, the more upset we become and this can lead to self-defeating or destructive behavior. If we follow the ABC plan, we find that with *less intense* upset feelings we are *less likely* to do self-defeating or destructive things!

Problem Solving with the ABCs

The second part of the ABCs has to do with problem solving. In going from A through D, we become less agitated with the situation by modifying our upsetting thinking. The second part of the ABCs deals with what we want to do about the problem situation itself (A). At D, we start to change our thinking about the situation by questioning our negative thoughts. Through this process, we begin to develop more realistic alternatives to our upsetting beliefs. This leads to the next part of the ABCs, which is "E," what we want to see happen regarding the situation.

"E" stands for expected new *realistic* goals. We set some positive goals to replace our unrealistic demands. We ask ourselves, "What about the situation can I change, and what will I have to accept?" The Serenity Prayer may be a guide in setting goals for yourself. You usually find that you can only change your own behavior and will have to accept other people's behavior. At (E) in the ABCs, you develop some realistic goals for problem situations.

Following are some examples of changing upsetting beliefs (B) to more realistic or positive goals (E). These may be helpful and familiar. Common distressing thoughts

cause many people to have upset feelings.
1) "I *must* have love or approval from everyone for everything I do. I *should* please everyone. I *should* have everyone's love." We see here the self-centered demand for acceptance and approval. Anxiety and depression usually result from this unrealistic demand. This upsetting belief, "People *must* love and approve of me" might be changed to a more realistic goal: "It would be better if people loved or approved of me. The acceptance and approval of others is desirable but not absolutely necessary."
2) "To be worthwhile, I *should* be competent, adequate, and achieving in all respects. I *must* not make mistakes or do poorly; making mistakes is *awful.* I *should* be perfect." The demand is for perfection. Like the example above, the result of this unrealistic demand is depression or anxiety. This upsetting belief might be changed to: "Doing things well is satisfying but it is human to make mistakes. I will strive for success and learn from failures."
3) "People and situations *should* always be the way I want them to be. People *should* behave differently. They *should* do it my way. I *must* be right." Demanding one's own way or needing to control are seen here. The result of this upsetting belief is anger. The demand that "People *should* behave the way I want them to" might be changed to: "While I may prefer that someone behave differently, I may have to accept their behavior realizing that acceptance does not necessarily mean liking or approving."

At (E) in the ABCs we set more realistic goals for ourselves to replace upsetting, unrealistic demands. Each of us will differ somewhat in our goals; however, sobriety will remain our basic goal in every problem situation. If new goals are not going to help maintain sobriety, then we had better revise our goals!

Once we set some positive goals, how do we reach them? This brings us to (F) in the ABC format. "F" stands for facilitating methods in which we look for *constructive actions* we can take to achieve our new realistic goals (E). Frequently, these constructive methods will involve both talking and listening. For example, if your goal was to argue less with your spouse, the method used might be openly expressing concerns to your spouse and listening to his or her concerns in return. Other constructive methods involve social skills, assertion skills, and acceptance behavior. When looking for constructive methods, it is important to be concrete and to describe specific actions that can be taken. Keeping actions simple and specific makes them easier to perform.

When we begin to apply part (F) of the ABCs, we may be at a loss to think of constructive actions since we have viewed things so negatively in the past. Friends may be of particular help in suggesting possible constructive methods since they view our problem situations from a different perspective. Asking for assistance is another way of practicing Step 2 of AA and it reinforces the hope for change.

The final part of the ABC format is (G). At (E), we set some new realistic goals for ourselves and at (F) we discovered some different methods to help reach these goals. "G" stands for application, that is, taking positive action to achieve our goals.

At point (G) we select the best methods (F) of achieving our goals (E) and then *do* them. Oftentimes this will mean practicing the application of these methods since this may involve a new way of behaving. In this final phase of the ABCs, we learn to take constructive positive action to solve problem situations rather than the old destructive or self-defeating actions of the past which were a part of the unmanageability of our upset feelings.

Goal achievement is reached through persistent, hard work. The positive outcome, however, reinforces constructive behavior and encourages us to continue to take positive action in problem situations.

With the setting of new realistic goals (E) and the application (G) of constructive actions (F) we demonstrate our decision to change. The application of constructive goals and actions is a demonstration of "letting go" of the need to control and a willingness to "turn it over." The application of constructive actions involves turning to others for help and change rather than always trying to control. This is consistent with Step 3 of AA.

The ABC process provides us with a way to take a personal inventory as a part of Step 10 of AA. The ABC process is a problem-solving approach for reducing upset feelings and behaving responsibly. It is a way of dealing with strong upset feelings or those distressing feelings that hang on. The ABC process allows us to reduce or modify upset feelings, not do away with them altogether. It is human to be upset!

Some Examples of Using the ABCs

The following are some examples of how the ABC process might be used to deal with upset feelings triggered by our upsetting thoughts.

Example 1:
1) The situation (A) is having to give a talk in front of a group.
2) I'm feeling very tense and anxious (C).
3) I ask myself, "What am I telling myself? (B) I *shouldn't* make any mistakes." Perfectionism is evident here.
4) I start questioning (D) my upsetting thinking: "What is so awful about making mistakes? Nothing. It is human to make mistakes. Stop being a perfectionist!"
5) I then change my upsetting beliefs to more realistic goals (E), such as "I would like to give my talk with as few mistakes as possible."
6) I make a list of possible constructive actions (F): (1) practice my talk; (2) apply Step 3 of AA, telling myself to turn it over; and (3) tell myself repeatedly to calm down and not get so upset. By doing this I am sending myself positive messages rather than the old negative upsetting thoughts.
7) I then select one or more of the constructive methods and put them into action (G).

Example 2:
1) The situation (A): I had a slip and started drinking.
2) I'm feeling depressed and guilty (C).
3) What am I telling myself? (B) "I am a bad person for not being able to control my drinking and I can't change."

4) I start questioning my negative thinking (D). "Remember, alcoholism is viewed as a disease. Being powerless does not make me a morally bad person. Who says I can't change? I am the one that is saying that. Change is difficult but not impossible. Many others have done it."
5) My goal (E) is to accept Step 2 of AA: "Came to believe that a Power greater than ourselves could restore us to sanity."
6) The method (F) that I might use to realize the goal of Step 2 would be to share my thoughts and feelings with peers about my alcoholism and listen to what they have to say.

How do we know when to use the ABCs to take a Step 10 personal inventory? When we realize that we're getting upset. The ABC process helps as follows:

1) Identify upset feelings (C). These feelings are clues that you are telling yourself negative things. Use these upset feelings as *stop signs!* They are a signal that it may be time to take a personal inventory.
2) Counteract your upsetting thoughts with a *positive self-message*. Say to yourself, "Slow down, easy does it. Don't get so upset."
3) Clarify the situation for yourself. Take a careful look at the problem situation (A). Ask yourself, "What is *really* going on in the situation about which I became upset? What are *facts* and what are *opinions*?"
4) Identify your upsetting thoughts (B). Ask "What am I telling myself?" Here is where you identify the "shoulds," the "I can'ts," the "awfuls," and the self-blaming.
5) Question (D) your upsetting thoughts (B). Ask yourself "Why?", "Who said so?", "Where is my

evidence?" And then *answer* the questions.
6) Change your unrealistic distressing thoughts to realistic new goals (E). Ask yourself, "What do I really want out of the situation?" Remember the Serenity Prayer. "What about the situation can I change? What will I need to accept?" Change or acceptance in regard to the situation become goals.
7) Find constructive methods or actions (F) you could take to achieve your new goals (E). Make a list of all possible constructive actions.
8) Decide which goal to work on, then choose a constructive option and put it into practice (G). After looking at the probable outcome of each action, select the one that will have the best pay-off. The result of the ABC process is a positive self-image which will reflect in your actions.

Summary

As we have seen, upsetting thinking leads to upset feelings and then to self-defeating or destructive behavior. The ABC format provides a way of coping with upset feelings. The ABC process is a method to help us develop more self-awareness and it relates directly to Steps 1, 2, 3, and 10 of AA. In using the ABCs, we learn to identify upset feelings and their consequences of self-defeating or destructive behavior which includes the use of alcohol or other drugs. We have learned to identify and modify the negative thinking which is the basis of upsetting thinking. Thinking more realistically allows us to set more realistic goals and, in turn, cope more positively and deal more constructively with everyday problems.

Sobriety has been described as not using alcohol or other drugs and seeing things differently. The ABC format may be of assistance to you in maintaining your sobriety because it helps you to see things differently.

The ABC Process

A = SITUATION *(activating event):* Something happens or is about to happen. The situation about which you are having some emotional feelings.

B = THOUGHTS *(belief system):* Your beliefs, thoughts, or attitudes about the situation (A). What you tell yourself.

C = FEELINGS *(emotional consequences):* Your emotional reactions as a result of your thoughts or beliefs (B). How you feel.

C_b = ACTIONS *(behavioral consequences):* What you do as a result of your feelings (C). How you behave or act.

D = QUESTIONING *(disputing the upsetting beliefs):* Challenging or questioning your thinking (B). You identify and question that which is unrealistic or upsetting in your thinking. Modifying your upsetting thoughts or beliefs.

E = GOALS *(expected new realistic goals):* Setting goals for yourself regarding the situation (A). Realistic alternatives to your upsetting beliefs (B).

F = FACILITATING METHODS *(constructive actions):* Ways to reach your realistic goals (E).

G = APPLICATION *(goal achievement):* Putting into practice your decision to change.

Practice Pages

Think of one example in which you might have used the ABC process and carry it out on the following practice pages. The more you practice, the more natural this thinking will become.

Instructions: Fill out the sections in this order: A first, then C, then C$_b$, then B, then D, E, F and G.

A = The Situation: Describe a situation about which you became upset. Keep it simple, stating just the basic facts.

B = Thoughts: Write out your upsetting beliefs or thoughts about the situation. Number and list each one separately below. Identify your "shoulds," "awfuls," "I can'ts," and examples of self-blaming.

C = Feelings: Describe the upset feelings you had in regard to the situation. Were you feeling depression, anxiety, fear, anger, or guilt?

C_b = Actions: Describe the way you behaved, what you did, as a result of the upset feelings. What was the outcome of your actions?

D = Questioning: Write out your questioning of each upsetting belief. Write the questions in order of the corresponding belief in (B). Ask yourself "Who said so?", "Where is my evidence or can I prove it?", "Why?" Then answer the questions.

E = Goals: List your expected new realistic (reachable) goals for the situation. (If you have more than one goal, list your goals by number in order of priority.) What about the situation can you change? What will you have to accept? Change your *demands* to *desires,* from "should" to "it would be better" or "I would prefer."

F = Methods: List the specific methods or possible constructive actions you could take to reach your goals. (List the constructive actions or methods according to the number of your goals above.)

G = Applications: List the goal(s) you chose and the constructive action(s) that you took. Describe how you felt and what happened as a result of the constructive actions you took.

Practice Pages

Think of another example in which you might have used the ABC process and carry it out on the following practice pages. The more you practice, the more natural this thinking will become.

Instructions: Fill out the sections in this order: A first, then C, then C$_b$, then B, then D, E, F and G.

A = The Situation: Describe a situation about which you became upset. Keep it simple, stating just the basic facts.

B = Thoughts: Write out your upsetting beliefs or thoughts about the situation. Number and list each one separately below. Identify your "shoulds," "awfuls," "I can'ts," and examples of self-blaming.

C = Feelings: Describe the upset feelings you had in regard to the situation. Were you feeling depression, anxiety, fear, anger, or guilt?

C$_b$ = Actions: Describe the way you behaved, what you did, as a result of the upset feelings. What was the outcome of your actions?

D = Questioning: Write out your questioning of each upsetting belief. Write the questions in order of the corresponding belief in (B). Ask yourself "Who said so?" "Where is my evidence or can I prove it?", "Why?" Then answer the questions.

E = Goals: List your expected new realistic (reachable) goals for the situation. (If you have more than one goal, list your goals by number in order of priority.) What about the situation can you change? What will you have to accept? Change your *demands* to *desires,* from "should" to "it would be better" or "I would prefer."

F = Methods: List the specific methods or possible constructive actions you could take to reach your goals. (List the constructive actions or methods according to the number of your goals above.)

G = Applications: List the goal(s) you chose and the constructive action(s) that you took. Describe how you felt and what happened as a result of the constructive actions you took.

Suggested Readings

Anderson, Daniel J. *Anxiety/Conflicts and Chemical Dependency.* Center City, Minnesota: Hazelden Educational Services. 1976.

Ellis, A. & Harper, R. A. *A New Guide to Rational Living.* No. Hollywood, Ca.: Wilshire, 1975.

Jensen, James G. *Another Look at Step One.* Center City, Minnesota: Hazelden Educational Services. 1972.

Jensen, James G. *Step Three: Turning It Over.* Center City, Minnesota: Hazelden Educational Services. 1980.

Jensen, James G. *Step Two: A Promise of Hope.* Center City, Minnesota: Hazelden Educational Services. 1980.

Jordan, William George. *Majesty of Calmness.* Center City, Minnesota: Hazelden Educational Services. 1980.

Kranzler, G. D. *You Can Change How You Feel.* New York: Institute for Rational Living, 1975.

Maultsby, M. C., Jr. *Help Yourself to Happiness.* Boston: Marlborough, 1975.

Maultsby, M. C., Jr., *A Million Dollars for Your Hangover.* Kentucky: Rational Self-Help Books, 1978.

Springborn, William. *Step One: The Foundation of Recovery.* Center City, Minnesota: Hazelden Educational Services. 1977.

The ABC Process

A = SITUATION *(activating event):* Something happens or is about to happen. The situation about which you are having some emotional feelings.
B = THOUGHTS *(belief system):* Your beliefs, thoughts, or attitudes about the situation (A). What you tell yourself.
C = FEELINGS *(emotional consequences):* Your emotional reactions as a result of your thoughts or beliefs (B). How you feel.
C_b = ACTIONS *(behavioral consequences):* What you do as a result of your feelings (C). How you behave or act.
D = QUESTIONING *(disputing the upsetting beliefs):* Challenging or questioning your thinking (B). You identify and question that which is unrealistic or upsetting in your thinking. Modifying your upsetting thoughts or beliefs.
E = GOALS *(expected new realistic goals):* Setting goals for yourself regarding the situation (A). Realistic alternatives to your upsetting beliefs (B).
F = FACILITATING METHODS *(constructive actions):* Ways to reach your realistic goals (E).
G = APPLICATION *(goal achievement):* Putting into practice your decision to change.